RUMMAGES ACROSS THE DEAD LAND

Book IV

THE MAGIC MAN

For the memory of my Father—a man
of euphoric mind and boundless spirit—Dr. Argha Banerjee.

••• ••• •••

Contents

●●● ●●● ●●●

The Mourner's Writ

It is
to run slower,
to walk
at the pace
of despair.. that
moves to surround
and devour the whole
of what keeps
the mind.

It is
to not just be
haunted.. but also
to face
the hollows..
collect
the roar from winds..
patterns from thunder..
to hold still ..the rustle
betwixt cold fingers, and
try
to spell
a picture.

A Trace

An essence
of something... unmistakable more
than
our mortality,
lingered.. in the perfume of his study.

What Next?

Is too much
of a bad question
to ask
a thinking-man,
who mostly
spends most
of the next moment
somewhere... in the past;
for the past,
in experiencing,
was… reality, in
reliving is unreality
of dreams…
while a future..
a lone eventuality - in all of now,
is inscrutable myth!
for hardly
do dreams
entail a future.

Will-o'-the-wisp

It's strange
how...
in the homelike refuge
of a single inelaborate dream...

it is too easy
to dismantle, on pure instinct,
and thereby dismiss

what you
somewhere.. still
remember to be
the unshakable dominion
of the sum
of unforgiving reality..

as simply, the absurd deceit
of an unimportant nightmare

within a dream.

Echoes of Disquiet

I'm glad that one old man
remembers to take his medicine.
He tends
to speak very little
these days
and the few words that surface,
are sometimes, a solemn source
of sad comfort.
The other day, we happened
to discover
a mutual guilt…
in possibilities of
a few things
we might have done different… to thus,
have deferred the routes
to two abrupt terminals.. of a kindred loss - in
our divergent histories, that
since then... cannot matter.

But it is
at times ..unnerving
to know that one is the last
of a particular kind of blood,
and has failed irrevocably..! to protect those
who had always protected him.

Therefore,
it remains
to gaze upon reflection
and search for traces
of faces bygone, where one might
imagine reflexively.. for
the dwindling remainder
of the cherished few... as much as for the self:
how the face, the lowered eyelids,
low breathing, tired arms,
restive legs,
the twitching.. in all,
would be rendered
- when devoid
of the animus of consciousness - of the spark of
life..
then
left alone for days, to rot..!!

and
in these forsaken hours
of insomnious nightmare..
can one glimpse.. the ruthless truth
of the nature and eventuality of this raw flesh..
can see right through seductive illusions
of presence... and mistakes
of love and hope.

Unrealizing Hope

I wish,
most foolishly, that
it eludes you..
that you somehow escape..
and it never
comes to pass... that reality,
in impersonal manifestation,
leaves
the brightest
of all dreams
upturned, without warning,
as a figment, an
illusion without possibility; except.. in
red moments of desperate madness. And
it remains too low
to crave
the obliviousness of beasts,
and despicable of our nature
that time
is meant to submerge
even that One brightest
of dreams.

Hunted

At times,
I find myself running
away from all the things
that remind me of you…
or more,
the ubiquity
of what is now the absence
of your shelter.

It is,
as if to attempt
escaping a labyrinth
of chasms.. left
inside this body,
and struggle
to slither off
this build of hollowed bone.

Can't run for long..
and there is no place
to go to..
to save the remains
of the mind,
where respite is lack
of consciousness:
to slip into,

past your living pictures
that wander
about this head..
and
tear away!
with a distinct.. echo
of your distant… searching.. call.

No solace
lives
in memory.

The bad
is that
we never ..imagined.

The good
is what   is lost.

Excuse

It doesn't feel
as if Time
has already begun
to eat away,
to dull and coldly
anaesthetize the pangs
of the immitigable finality
of this vacuum.

It's just
that this bitch of a life!
doesn't let you
stand still...
and there was too much
raw sewage! pointless shit - to look into
today, as there was
the
last
time
you called
to ask if
I was coming
that day,
and I said
that I'd come
that weekend, and
asked if
you were feeling
alright, if

you were feeling
tired...
to which,
after a long
pause,
you replied
that you felt
very... tired...
and I asked
of you,
for the
last
time... to rest... and
you
listened.

And again...
there was too much
of all this today, as there
may be
for who knows
how many hollow tomorrows...
to let me
get lost
in visions
of
'you'.

Stigma

And when I
still had... the chance,
you hardly asked.. for what
I knew
I should've been more… for you;
and I didn't
take enough
care...
of you.. and I wasn't
the only one. So,
now I keep reminding
not just myself, but
also the few
who should have,
and I might just be killing
us all.

Gauze

It doesn't help..!
this irate
and bitter writing in powerless agony.

Like alcohol,
it doesn't dull
that ..sinking
feeling one gets
on disinterring
an indispensable
image..
that no longer
exists
in places
other than the heart.

At least cheap
whisky, in a while,
fogs the senses
and knocks you cold... while
..a metamorphosis of despairing thoughts to disquiet
expression..
in contrariety,
keeps you waking
and alert
as in excision without anesthetics,

at times... with words
to stopple
too much bleeding.

Noise

It
will
get
better.

Let time heal.

Stop torturing yourself!

You need to pick yourself back up.
There's nothing more you could've done.
There's no way that you could've known.
This isn't something we can change.

You'll start to drive yourself insane..

You can't give up.
You can't break down.
You cannot just
d i s i n t e g r a t e.

You can't just keep thinking.
can't just keep brooding.
can't just keep bleeding.

There's nothing more that you could do…

YEAH WELL YOU KNOW WHAT, FUCK YOU TOO!!!

I know I still got work to do.
As what he would have said to you.

Denying the Flies

Didn't see
it coming; not
that I couldn't; just
didn't. Didn't
want to.
No one wants to;
not when it matters...
no one wants
to have seen it, even
if they could.. even
when they knew.. or at least

foresaw
an onrushing wake of mistakes.. and
closing probabilities.

No one's ready
to see
when they figure
it might
turn out exactly
how they expected and refused
to acknowledge,
in ..disbelieving fear.. and...
no one
is really
prepared.

Deficit

Were words not overused
as they are,
perhaps
there would be more dignity
in 'grief',
that is to say,
the vicissitudes of turbulence
in the ravaged valley of the 'heart',
that serves
as contemptible metaphor
for the entirety of one's substance
susceptible to 'despair',
the kind
that makes you despise
the glass half-full
and envy
the sound of 'laughter'
made in blissful ignorance
of the barbarity
of cold 'time',
which is,
as Dad used to say,
just "a unit
  used to measure
  the changes
  of nature".

What If?

It's hard
to cloud the closure..
and remember just
the fullness of good
in what
you had become.

The irony in mind,
remains the spectacle.. the sound
of your resounding laughter!
in innocence
of impending inevitability.

This failure
isn't
reversible, as are
so many
benumbing things, in wading
these shallows of unimportance.
Yet..
dreams arrive
in waking, to transpire
as madness
of impossible abstractions
on concealed sources
and conspiring possibilities..?

Ones of Twos

It should
begin in twos:
your worlds - for you, upon
a time, until one
is gone.. and
it doesn't hurt at all..!
as long
as you've forgotten
that there's no longer
one completely familiar
place... you can always... at
any of all times, come 'home'
to - to complete safety...
and then
it all collapses
and impales you sharper and deeper..!
each time - like drowning again
and again,
in colder
and colder currents
of blinding, pitch-black snow.

Thereafter,
the fullness of the world:
the last
of your first, in the one
remaining other... would,
on another unexceptional day,

disappear..

and
you'd find
you're old overnight
and may have already
become one - yourself.

Towrope

Whatever
'is' - exists
entirely in the mind; and
would be absent in entirety
if erased
from it. And
any lingering presence
in the world outside, would
be rendered new,
strange
and alien to memory.

Annihilation
of just one's memory
would entail
the complete excision of the individual
from the existence of the other.

And memory:
even inaccessible
or repressed - would
be key,
as wellspring
to engender... old existence - if
mined, disinterred and wrought
as newer life..

Wishful Thinking

These days
are strange as the nights,
where I can't help revisiting
the absurdity.. of your defeat..

And
it seems, then,
a rather good idea
to visit some
snow - an evening
with a small handgun,
have it loaded, listen
for the 'click' - as
the hammer's cocked; then
hold it backwards,
point the barrel
right down between
the eyes - straight up
the middle, and gently
slip a calm thumb
before the easeful trigger,
lean delectably into
the freezing metal muzzle..
grin..   pull..

BANG!!!
.. ..
.

And it's all fixed..
it all... gets better...
it all
goes back the way
it was always
meant
to be:

no lights
and no more
fucking eVERYTHing!! up..

to
end up nowhere...
unconscious of being
with you.

Incarnate

To extract
from
the coils of my existence,
the strings, the double-helix
of
your being...

and
imprint it
with the quintessence of every memory
you left
in me.

mantra

She said
I spoke to you.. while
ailing and delirious, and I remember
what I was saying,
but can't recall hearing
the sound of your voice, nor feeling
an air of your presence - at all, at
the time, except
for a part
of an unfinished sentence, on
an obscure page of a much-unused diary,
where you wrote
that the discovery
of your life
had been
that you were wrong...

and I wanted
to finish the sentence
in writing: you
were loved... you are remembered...

yet all my demons held me there
as I kept murmuring in hopeless delirium..
as if to answer
an expected question:
"yes I am a part of you"
"yes I am a part of you"
"yes I am a part of you"
"yes I am a part of you"

A Madman's Wager

If 'impossible'
is myth
and 'inevitability'
is just a word,

then
maybe, just
maybe..

someone
will have the chance
to tell somebody,
someday...

that "you
are everything I could have salvaged
of you".

Where the Two of Them Watched Late-night Movies, While I Fell Asleep

It came
late last night:
a vision
of perhaps... the safest of places
from those early, freer years that
then dried up
and hardened as burnt-brown earth..
to something
long-suspended, poorly preserved and
somehow... I felt it
observe me intently,
in
the saddest of ways...
before crumbling altogether
into the dirt.

Like Father, Like Son

Down the lines
to slow
estrangement... till
I'd move into
a one-room apartment
close to work
and closer to travel, with
barely a window, hardly a view and
seldom have it mopped, but
have those shirts
dry-cleaned and routinely pressed,
reread escaping books,
revisit reruns and
stranger passing screens among
the angles.. each
wall makes
with the same ceiling.. and
in time, get restless and visit
a whore
or two - which
I'm not sure you
did, but
only get lonelier... to turn
to the reeds, needles and white;
then quit the drugs,
then give up whisky,
then stop smoking and
try
starving
from time

to time to test
how much I can take, though
I doubt I'd be able to do it
as well
as you did.

No saints
you and I, but
each of us
belonged... to
a woman, whom
we mistreated
in our different ways, as
they did
in theirs, and
it seemed
that everyone learned
to live
by themselves, though
it's us - you
and I, who couldn't
or can't
care or smile
as much
for ourselves
at
all.

Flipbook

Still
everyday
I see you in waking,
in all your varied temperaments,
that
flash before
and past these eyes insatiable
for the frenzied meanderings
of a wounded mind.

Dispossession

You knew
that I looked somewhat
like you, and
lately I find you
in so many ways
I sound
and act
and where
we come from, they might
just say that
a part of you
must've latched on to me
the last time
I held
your.. fingers
and I'd kill for it to be True..!! but
I recollect... that
I was
this way
for as long as I can
remember, and
just didn't realize
it
sooner... to
see
how a lot of me died
with you.

Echo

I thought
to myself yesterday
that just like it was
before, you probably wouldn't
have agreed to listen
to my many trifling tales
of weakness
and petty failures,
just like you never shared
your harder stories
with me, unlike
you did with her, my
mother, who once
used to be
your friend... and
once divulged to me,
one of your secrets. And I saw
that you neither spoke,
nor sought to listen because
you were
too ashamed to reveal
your scars and
too proud to believe that
I might have a few
of my own...

Perhaps...
you didn't want us
to become as alike
as we

turned out to be.

Perhaps...
you didn't want me
in some places
you used
to be.

Dead Salvage

And soon
I'll sell the old house
that used to be
our home... but
first I've got to get.. his books out..
to save..
his leftover clothes,
his flip-flops, two shoes,
three tables, chairs,
an induction cooker,
an iron trunk, the small TV,
the memories..
and mounted eulogies of our guardians...
the walking stick
he kept
from his father, who
was swallowed there as well.
I think
I'll burn his
lone bed, the one
where I used to sleep
as a child
betwixt its parents, so
that no one else
touches it!

The Last of Places

When
his mother died
and I watched them hoist
her large, irresilient frame
upon the pyre,
bare betwixt red sheets,
I was too little
to realize
that she'd never speak to me... again.

Then,
when it was time
for his father, and
they did away with
the worn, decrepit shape,
the same way
they had
for his wife, I
understood... that
I'd see them both again..
someday... in a place
we all go upon
our wanting, ashen ends.

And...
as I

set fire
to his remains.. the
ruin.. that had become of my father..
I had already
arrived at the deliberation
that mind
cannot outlive
the disorganization of its matter,
that oblivion
is akin
to the restful nothingness
of an eternal, dreamless sleep...
and that
the only place
where we
could all be alive... together...
was in the imprecision
of fading memories.

A Reunion

Pessoa said
that *to write*
is to forget, and
I didn't believe him, until
it started to soothe
the burning
of times bygone... which
were now meant for revisiting, at
times in rain, and
among other opiates, words, as tunnels
or doors
to inhumed realities; and
it somehow
was more pleasant
to remember the loved absent...
at the best
of what they were...
until.. a long-lost photograph
of a long-dead, old man
retrieved the lifeless face
of your father - my friend, our guardian
left almost as in weeping.. from
what I know
was so much left unfinished... but
what now.. impossibly feels.. from
a sorrow grasped
before the living: when
once again, I'm cut wide open.. as

you turn

to the mingling of your sources, and
whelmed within their realm of nonbeing,
you appear now, to me, betwixt
the living and motionless figures
of your two grand guardians... poised,
in my mind,
before and diminishing a great darkness!

with they,
as now you,
at the most beautiful
of what remains in memory...
with me? left here - behind and alone to envision
you all
and suffer
on my own;
never
to say
goodbye.

The Perfect Blue

The idea
of Paradise, as
a place
where the ideal
is reality... seems
something we'd like
to imagine
as going somewhere
that was dreamed or envisioned,
or once, really was.. immaculate…

and some place
we usually know,
can no longer be
as perfect, on arrival
there.

The last time
we saw each other,
we spoke
of his childhood
in a boarding school,
where mornings came before
the sun, at times
before the break of dawn
and then,
there was routine for some
chosen, in clearing dust

from prayer halls, and watering
the stretches of flowers that
lined the grounds, before
the other children
were up.

I assumed
it must have been tiring
to rise so early, each day,
and then do that much work,
to which,
to my surprise,
he said
that he used to enjoy it,
and explained
that the feel
of fresh, open air...
that bathed the body,
and the gleam
of that dim, first light... that
illumined the skies
would allow
his young mind
to be lively! and
free...

It's difficult
at times, to tell
dreams from reality..
but I know

I asked if he
would like to revisit
those faraway gardens
once again... one
early morning, with me
this time.

Or was I..
just waiting
for the next time
I'd see him..
and only dreamed
that I had already
asked..?

Someone told me
that life
is supposed to be
a procession...
of
unbearable passing..
and I claimed that it would've
been better
to never have
existed, but once
one does...
there's too much
to try
to hold near, to simply
go away...
until we bid adieu
to Heaven... that hides

in the impossibility
of complete return
to the elusive fulfillment
of some mysterious places
on this uncaring earth.

Elitist Listener

Is finding
music
that, for a long
few minutes,
fills
the hollows...
that
one cannot
touch - inside...
enough
of a reason
to stay
alive?

There are
many
more important
ones, where
the well-being
of another
becomes
of more
consequence
to you, than your own.

Perhaps

a child, for whom
his Dad
gave up his drugs
and
worked hard
to give the delinquent
an education.

Or a personal purpose,
as a brilliant and unsuccessful doctor
rereading repurchased books
of Pathology,
to redress
an age neglected,
in the waning hope
of restoring
an out-of-reach laboratory,
and dying
of a heart attack
at forty-nine,
confused.. and alone..
while
the kid, now a man, the
one thing
he wholeheartedly cherished...
was out
making money
somewhere in the big fucking city!

For those

who do not believe
in fairy tales
and have seen their share
of futile trial
and cruel death,
it suffices to say
that
they often find
little reason to feel
that reality
was ever directed
toward
anything good,
and… eventually has
no meaning, other
than sadder memories.

And
in this capricious state
of the definite
and oncoming nature
of unpredictable
and irrevocable loss..
perhaps,
discovering pointless music
that makes you think
such pointless thoughts,
is as good a reason as any... for
lingering, pathetically, here.

For all reason,
in time,
disappears..
in one inescapable vacuum..
and is rendered
unknown,
unknowable,
null
and
void.

While the ravages
of mortality
tend
to take the shine
away
from dreams,
it is, or still feels
wrong
to take
one's own life,
as long
as there are those you'd hurt,
were you
to simply
go away.

Someone
had once
asked

my father
what he wanted
his son
to be, when I
grew up.
To this,
the M.D. Pathologist
replied:
"Alive and Happy"
...and that
is what I'll
try...
to be.

Will and Testament

You never said
what I should do
now..

so, I'll do
the things
you wanted
to, and
get everything! that
you desired, and strive...
to act in ways
that
would then have made you happy...

The Magic Man

July 13.
It's already
been
a month, and
today
is still...
your birthday.

You know...?

for a few
grey weeks,
I've been writing
for you.

I never
told you, but
I used to
think, when I
was little, that you
would be the grand nemesis
I would oppose
when I grew up.

But
somehow,
as I grew taller
midst the fall of our guardians,

you found
their secret..
and became
their last.

And
taught,
by your own example,
that human beings
are capable
of magic... of good... of change.

●●● ●●● ●●●

Cover art created in collaboration with my friend and artist, Subhra Kumar Banerjee.

Lightning Source UK Ltd.
Milton Keynes UK
UKHW040608280519
343447UK00001B/189/P

9 781389 563614